I'm Reading About

MONTANA

Big Sky Country!

GALLOPADE

by Carole Marsh

Printed and Manufactured in Peachtree City, GA., USA
www.gallopade.com

Book design: John Hanson

Editorial manager: Janice Baker

Montana is a great state.

It is one of a kind.

What makes Montana special?

Let's read about it and see!

NATIVE AMERICANS

Who lived in Montana first?

Native Americans did!

They moved around to find food.
They hunted in Montana's woods.
They fished in Montana's rivers.
They gathered fruits and seeds and nuts.

EXPLORERS

The first explorers came to Montana in 1805.
They came from the eastern United States.

Lewis and Clark were their leaders.
They were exploring new land!

The Louisiana Purchase included much of Montana.
The United States doubled in size after the Louisiana Purchase!

SETTLEMENT

Father Pierre Jean DeSmet came from Belgium to America.
He started the first settlement in Montana.
He named it St. Mary's Mission.

A mission was a place built to bring the Christian religion to the native people.

St. Mary's Mission

STATEHOOD

Montana was the 41st state
to join the United States of America!

Isn't it great,
to be a state!
I bet Montana
could hardly wait!

Montana became a state in 1889.

Montana
The 41st State

FLAG

I am the state flag.

What color am I?
I am blue.

Look at me.
What else do you see?

I fly high over the state of Montana!

MONTANA
ORO
-Y-
PLATA

CAPITAL

Say hello to Helena,
the capital city of Montana!

There is an important building in Helena.
It is the State Capitol.
Montana's laws are made there!

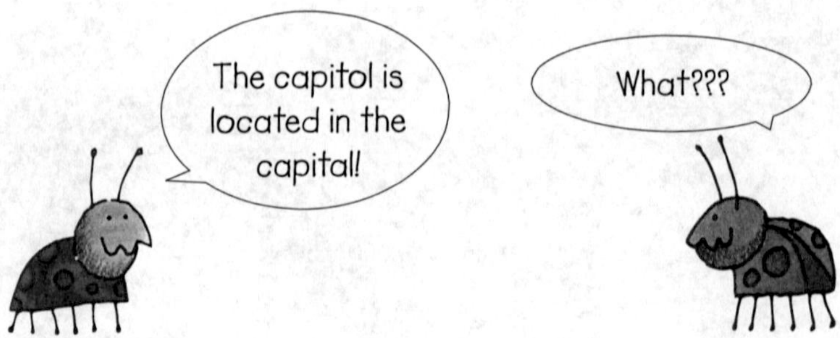

Capital

Capitol

SEAL

I am a seal,
but I am not the State Seal.
If I were, I would be very important.
I would be stamped on many official papers.
(Ouch, that might hurt!)

THE GREAT SEAL OF THE STATE OF MONTANA
ORO -Y- PLATA
Now, that's official!

NICKNAME

State nicknames are fun!
State nicknames are great!
They share fun facts
about each state!

One of Montana's nicknames is "Big Sky Country."

Montana's blue skies stretch as far as
the eye can see!

Big Sky Country

BORDERS

Look at Montana.
Montana is in a region called "the West."

Montana borders four other states.
It also borders the country of Canada.
Find Montana and its neighbors on the map!

Borders

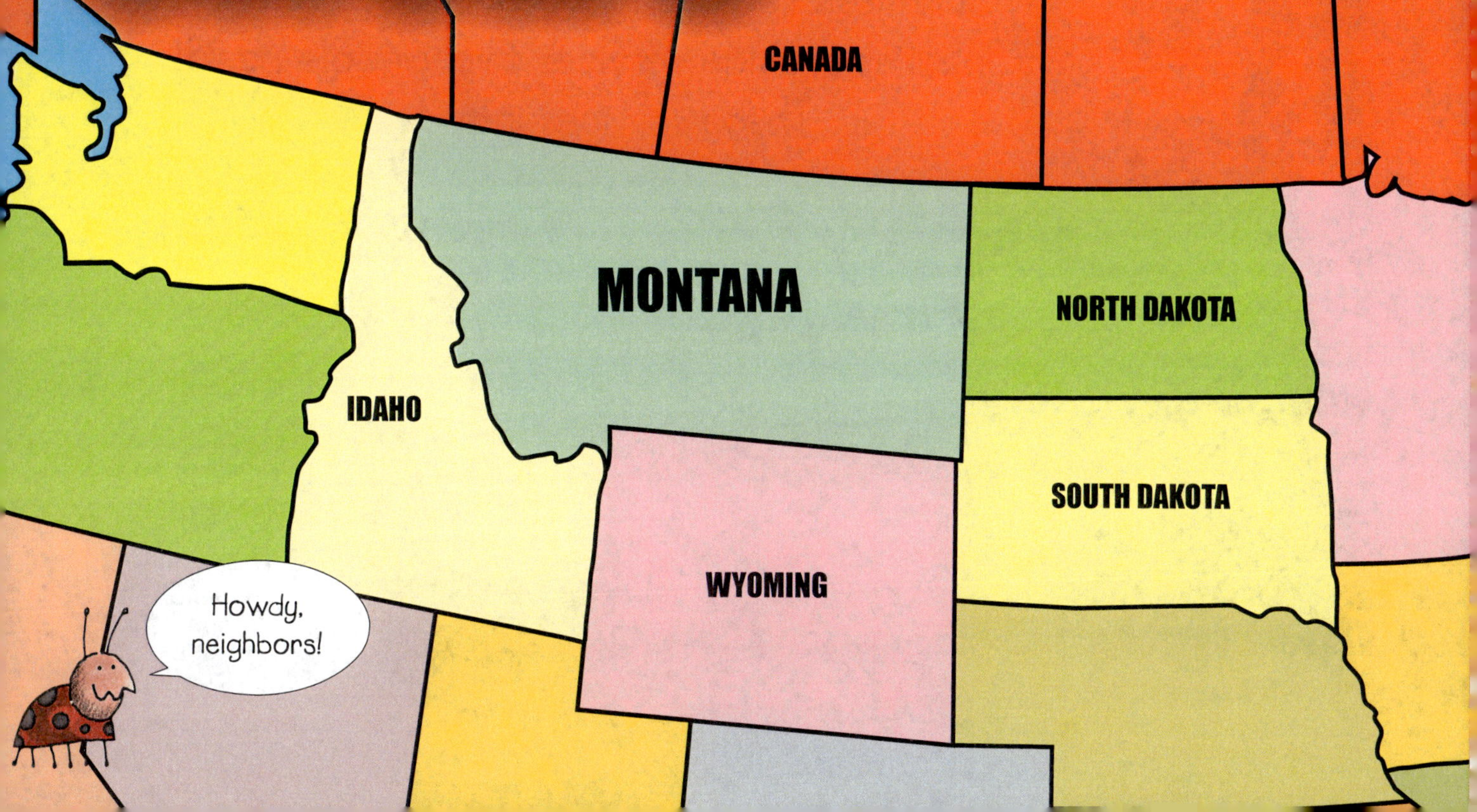
CANADA
MONTANA
NORTH DAKOTA
IDAHO
SOUTH DAKOTA
WYOMING
Howdy, neighbors!

COUNTIES

Montana is divided into 56 counties.
Counties are a form of local government.
Counties provide services that people need!
Those services include:

Schools **Parks** **Libraries** **Police**

Firefighters **and More!**

Counties

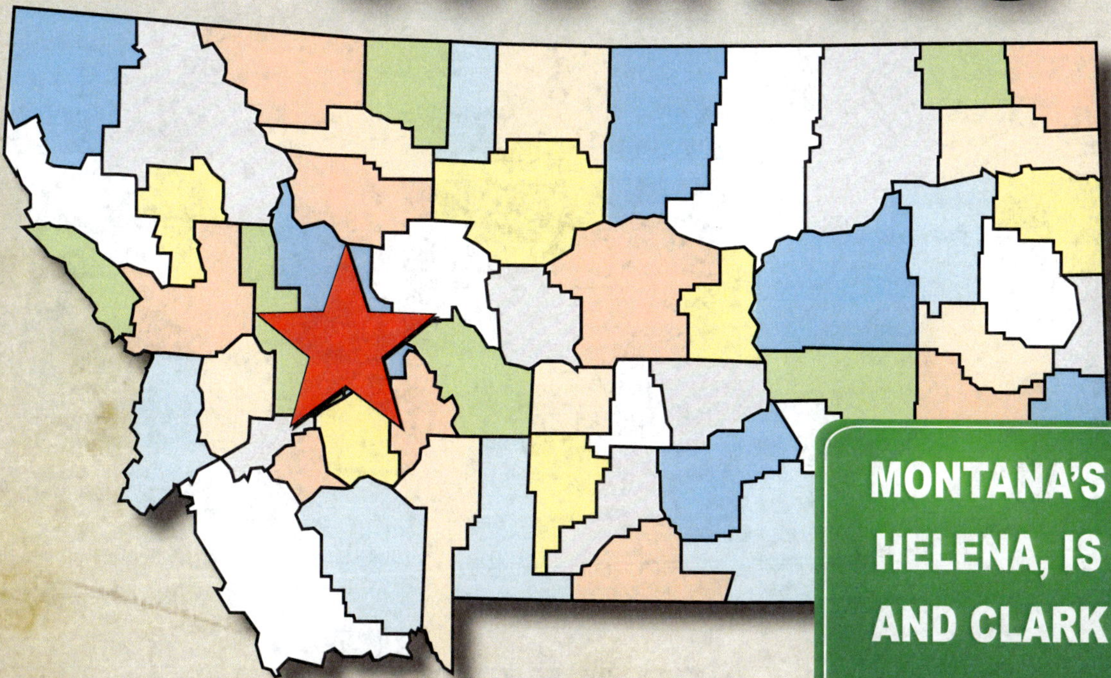

MONTANA'S CAPITAL, HELENA, IS IN LEWIS AND CLARK COUNTY.

PEOPLE

Many famous people

Charles Marion Russell

Artist of Western scenes often called the "Cowboy Artist"

Jeannette Rankin

First woman elected to the U.S. Congress (1916)

Maurice Hilleman

Scientist who developed vaccines for many serious illnesses

call our state home!

Let's hang out!

PEOPLE

Phil Jackson

Professional basketball coach whose teams won 11 NBA championships

Brad Bird

Animation artist who has worked on many movies, including *Ratatouille*

Eric Bergoust

Freestyle skier who won a gold medal in the 1998 Winter Olympics

Western Meadowlark

I am the state bird, and I fly
over Montana, proud and high.

As I fly, up in the sky,
I flap my wings to tell you "Hi!"

The Montana state bird is the Western Meadowlark.

BIRD

Bitterroot

FLOWER

I am the Bitterroot.
I am the state flower.

I grow where it's warm and sunny.
I bloom in spring and summer.
I help make Montana beautiful!

Look at me! Smell me!
Native Americans liked to eat
my roots.

Ponderosa Pine

TREE

I am a Ponderosa Pine—I'm the state tree.
All over Montana is where to find me.

My roots run deep, they keep me strong.
My leaves stay green, all year long.

I stand up straight, big and tall.
Don't climb too high—it would hurt to fall!

Mourning Cloak

I am the Mourning Cloak.
I am the state insect.

I flit and I fly from flower to flower.
I am looking for nectar to drink.

Look at my beautiful wings.
What colors do you see?

Prairies

PRAIRIES

Let's go to the prairie!

Montana has miles of prairies.
The tall golden grass sways in the breeze.

The prairie is flat,
There are no trees.
It stretches as far as the eye can see!

Montana's prairies are home to many animals:

Prairie Dogs **Badgers** **Coyotes** **Bison** **Deer** **and More!**

Rocky Mountains

MOUNTAINS

Montana's Rocky Mountains are the place to be.
Hiking, fishing, camping—
fun for you and me.

Winter weather brings lots of snow.
Temperatures drop to freezing and below!

Rivers

RIVERS

Montana has many rivers.
People like to use rivers for boating and fishing!

This habitat is home to many animals:

Birds Deer Snakes Frogs Fish and More!

The explorers Lewis and Clark used Montana's rivers to explore the area!

Glacier National Park

LANDMARK

Glacier National Park is a huge national park!
The park covers more than one million acres!
It spreads from the prairie to the tall Rocky Mountains.
Many plants and animals thrive in the park!

You can find grizzly bears, wolverines, and mountain goats in the park!

Montana Crops

Montana has many farms.
Why?
Because Montana has good soil and a mild climate!

Some of the top crops grown in Montana are:

Wheat **Hay** **Barley** **Sugarbeets**

Hey!
Don't forget about me!
Montana farmers raise lots of cattle, too.
Moooooooooo!

Sports in Montana

SPORTS

Baseball! Basketball! Football! Hockey!
Montana has it all.

Whether you like to watch or play,
You are sure to have a ball!

Grizzlies

Bobcats

Yellowjackets

& More!

Montana: The Treasure State

Montana is often called the "Treasure State." Miners found gold, silver, and copper in the state. A gold rush began in Montana in the mid 1800s! People "rushed" to Montana to find gold for themselves.

Many towns in Montana were built by the gold rush miners. Helena was once a "gold rush" town!

CLAIM TO FAME

GLOSSARY

animation: the process of making drawings or puppets look like they are moving

climate: weather conditions in an area over a long period of time

habitat: a place where plants or animals naturally live

laws: rules made by the government

nectar: a sweet liquid produced by plants, especially flowers

region: an area that has similar characteristics

settlement: the first community in an area

thrive: to grow or develop well

vaccine: a substance that is usually injected into a person or animal to protect against a particular disease